LOST IN THE ABYSS OF THOUGHTS

NAISHA KAUR

Made with ♥ on the Notion Press Platform
www.notionpress.com

Dedicated to all the lost souls trying to forge their paths

Contents

Acknowledgements

This book would not have been possible without the unwavering support and encouragement of the people around me.

To my mom, who ignited the spark of creativity within me. Being a talented writer herself, she inspired me to embrace my passion for writing. My dad has been my constant pillar of strength, always supporting me in my creative endeavors and encouraging me to follow my dreams.

I am incredibly grateful to all my teachers who nurtured my growth along the way. A special mention goes to my English teacher, Manoj Rawat Sir, whose guidance played a pivotal role in the publication of this book. His belief in me and his support throughout this journey made all the difference.

And of course, a shoutout to my friends—for not just being my partners in crime but for turning the melancholic poet in me into the sarcastic person I am today. If they find this acknowledgment boring, well... they know it's their job to roast me anyway.

Thank you all for being part of this journey and helping me bring this book to life.

Foreword

In the hands of a young poetess, there lies a delicate yet daring brush, painting with words the landscape of a soul still in bloom. As I turn the pages of this collection, I am struck not only by the tenderness of her musings but also by the wisdom they contain. Her poetry dances between the realms of the introspective and the universal, each poem a revelation of her inner journey as well as the collective human experience.

In My Soul, the poetess offers us a glimpse into the quiet chambers of her heart, while As My Ship Sails calls us to witness the voyage of self-discovery and courage. With a voice unapologetically her own, she declares in To Just Be Me the liberation found in authenticity. And when she weaves ancient myth into modern justice in Medusa: Unjust Justice, it is clear that her craft extends beyond her years, exploring the injustices that have been both lived and inherited.

Through poems like Voiceless Stories, Silenced by Glories and In Pursuit of Real Religion, she masterfully critiques the world with a pen that moves like a blade, soft and sharp in equal measure. She questions, she rebels, and she imagines new horizons.

This collection is not just an anthology of thoughts but a testament to the power of expression, unbound by convention yet deeply rooted in timeless truths. It is an honor to witness this young talent unfold her wings, for I believe, like the most enduring voices in literature, hers will soar far, inspiring generations to come.

I commend her for this beautiful collection, for in it lies the promise of a poetess who will leave an indelible mark on the literary world.

Manoj Rawat

(Pehlwanji)

Preface

Lost in the Abyss of Thoughts is a journey through the inner battles we often fight in silence. There are moments when the world seems to crash down on us, when everything feels unfair, unjust, and beyond reason. But in truth, the harshest battles are often the ones we fight within ourselves—against our thoughts, doubts, and fears—while no one seems to understand.

My intention in writing this book is to reach out to those who feel alone. I hope these poems resonate with them, offering a sense of familiarity and connection. For me, poetry has always been a source of purpose and peace, and I wish for readers to experience that same solace through these pages.

If even one person, through these words, embraces their doubts and realizes that hope is never far away, then this book will have achieved its purpose.

Thank you for joining me on this journey.

Questioning Everything

The book is divided into two parts:

1. Questioning Everything
2. Renaissance: The Revival Of Hope

Part 1 describes the dilemma one goes through in life. We all are expected to know our paths, make the right decisions, and be aware of our actions and future, but in reality, we don't know what we are doing! Life feels like a video being played repeatedly on a loop and we feel stuck and lost, that is where we all begin to question everything about life and get *lost in the abyss of thoughts...*

The only thing that rescues me from this abyss is poetry, my whole heart and soul.

1. Poetry: My Soul

Poetry, oh poetry, oh my true love!
My love for you soars beyond and above
You know my darkest side
In the most violent storms, you are my only guide
Oh! how I love to bleed on the paper
Unbeknownst to me, my tears turn into vapors
The way you express what I deeply feel,
The only way my heart heals
You've been with me all along
You are the reason, I stand strong
You glorified the pain
Beautified the blood stains
Only one who understood me without any bias
I can be my true self in this world of liars
Poetry screams at my face:

> "
>
> *Look at you comforting others with words you wish to hear*
> *Only she knows being left alone is my biggest fear*"

She isn't a part of me, she is me, I am her
The only element that fills my life with laughter

Poetry completes me as a whole
Poetry is my soul

The only reason I was motivated to write this book was poetry, it helped me survive the lonely days when I felt defeated and lost, poetry became a way for me to express my feelings. It gave me a sense of hope and direction. My sole purpose in writing this book is to offer solace through my poems, assuring every reader that they are not alone in their feelings and experiences.

2. As My Ship Sails!

Oh! it has been ages
Since I picked up a pen and got lost in the pages
Might be the first time I refused to write
The first time, when I didn't choose the light
So busy convincing myself everything was done
And all I could do was run,
From my own thoughts and emotions
I really tried escaping the commotion!
But it all came crashing down!
Once a fake smile, now just a frown,
Wondering where I lost myself?
Dust building on the memories I kept on the shelf
For, I buried my emotions alive!
Dead but they continued to thrive
It's a full-fledged garden now
That keeps poking my heart somehow,
Did I mention they were thorns and not flowers?
Brutal cold nights and not spring showers?
All these thorns but still emptiness prevails
I keep missing the shore *as my ship sails.*

I wrote this poem from a place of overwhelming confusion, feeling lost, completely lost to the point where the familiar things started feeling unfamiliar too. My home started feeling estranged from me. In a world where I'm supposed to know where I'm headed, I don't have a clue! I am on a journey, yes, but the path feels unclear, full of questions that leave me uncertain about my own emotions and destination. Burying them down in a deep dark corner of my heart, a place even I fear to tread. All I want is to escape, to silence the chaos, but it's as though no one truly understands.

I'm on this ship, sailing further from the shore, minute by minute, unsure if I'll ever find my way back. And as the distance grows, so does the fear—will I drown before I even reach my destination?

3. To Just Be Me

Sometimes I sit and wonder, what if my life was a book,
I am sure it would be complete chaos with too many hooks.
From childhood till now,
So many chapters have passed away somehow.
It feels nostalgic to read those pages again,
While some bring me pleasure and some bring me pain.
I hear my excited screams from the pages within,
A little girl who was eagerly hoping to win.
Win, in everything she wanted to pursue,
She won some, lost some, but every time learned something new.
Oh! those were the good old days,
The time when we had it our way.
Sometimes I wish to be her again,
The person so naive and unaware of the pain.
For she had the confidence to smile on the stage,
For her, self-doubt, insecurities, and judgments weren't a cage.
She is the person I still dream to be,
Oh god, what shall I do *to just be me*?

I find myself missing the person I used to be—the reason I speak of my past self in the third person, as "her," is because I no longer feel like that version of myself. She feels distant, almost like a stranger, someone I once knew but can no longer reach. I just miss the old version of me, someone I long to be…

She was never insecure about herself, she never questioned her potential, and she didn't cry late at night feeling completely desolated and lonely. She lived a free life, a way of living that I can never go back to, she did what she wanted to do, unstoppable, pure, and innocent away from the complexities of the world. She created her world and named it "Dreamtopia" obviously inspired by Barbie.

Every little achievement felt like a huge victory as if she had conquered the world and now, I have just lost the sense of achievement. A question that always strikes my mind is "Did I disappoint her?"

I wish for a time machine to take me back—to reclaim that purity, that simplicity, and just be... me again.

4. Medusa: Unjust Justice!

The epitome of beauty and purity
The one whose fate was blotched with obscurity
The one who sacrificed love,
For the goddess watching from above,
Goddess of wisdom, courage, justice and civilization
Goddess Athena was the one she loved beyond imagination!
Blessed with radiant hair that flowed like liquid gold,
Beauty so enchanting that it can neither be expressed nor told.
Ancient Greece echoed with her admiration,
But worshiping Athena was the path to her salvation
She became a priestess to worship the goddess,
Who knew it would lead to transgress?
The fate of a poor soul crushed between the fight,
Of the two immortals who wanted more might
Poseidon wanted to devastate Athena's glory
But why was Medusa dragged into this story?
Poseidon rose from the sea, his wrath a fierce tide
Seeking vengeance, Medusa's fate to decide
She ran towards Athena's temple seeking protection,
Hoping the goddess would repay her affection
Alas! The goddess turned a blind eye towards the poor soul
Poseidon succeeded in his motives so foul!
Medusa cried with agony and pain,

Athena finally came, not to console her but to punish her again!!
Athena's eyes filled with rage
Her precious temple was now an impure stage
Poor Medusa who thought Athena would console
Alas! Sought revenge from the wrong soul
Her temple's impurity
Was blamed on her beauty
She was turned into a gorgon with serpentine locks
Beauty turned to stone by a single glance from her toxic rocks,
Goddess of justice and wisdom herself, yet
blinded by rage, she neglected her wealth.
Hence the tale of the cursed priestess came into the notion
Until Perseus came to end the commotion...
This wasn't the last time, amidst two forces' hate,
An innocent faced a cursed fate
Needless to say,
As history repeats, justice is still served this way.

To understand this poem, you need to understand the story of Medusa [Greek Mythology]

"Medusa was a beautiful priestess who dedicated her life to Athena, the goddess of wisdom. (Medusa swore to remain a virgin to maintain her purity as a priestess). One day, Poseidon, the god of the sea, attacked her and sexually assaulted her in Athena's temple. Instead of protecting Medusa, Athena became angry that her temple was desecrated (impure) and punished Medusa (who was already the victim) by turning her into a Gorgon. This transformation made Medusa's once beautiful hair turn into snakes, and anyone who looked at her would turn to stone. Medusa, now a monster, lived in isolation, feared by everyone. Eventually, the hero Perseus was sent to defeat her as part of a quest. Armed with gifts from the gods, including a reflective shield, Perseus approached Medusa. He used the shield to avoid her deadly gaze, beheaded her, and took her head as a powerful weapon. Even in death, Medusa's head could still turn others to stone. Perseus's victory ended Medusa's tragic story, but it also served as a reminder of the injustice she faced."

Medusa's story just makes me so angry, it was Poseidon who was the real monster who attacked a priestess but alas it was Medusa who was punished for his sins.

This is not just some mythological story, this is the harsh reality even today the criminals escape and victims get punished for the crime that was committed to them.

Justice is still served this way…

The epitome of beauty and purityThe one whose fate was blotched with obscurity

5. Voiceless Stories, Silenced by Glory

It's been almost 8 decades since we became a free nation
Scared to go out after 8 PM, wow so much liberation!
Everyone is wearing the tricolour today
But I prefer to be adorned in black and grey
To mourn for the freedom we lost
Gained independence, but at what cost?
Dr. Moumita's death sends shivers down my spine
I want to scream a million words but I say I am just fine
We all hope for justice, what a waste of time
As in India, hoping for justice is a crime
Iss desh me insaaniyat bhul gye hai insaan
Bas gaana aata hai mera desh mahaan!
In the end, this will end up as a voiceless story
While pridefully, we'll keep celebrating the hollow glory

Context

Dr. Moumita, a postgraduate trainee at Kolkata's RG Kar Medical College, faced a tragic and brutal end in August 2024. She was discovered in a seminar hall, and the post-mortem revealed that she had been subjected to sexual assault and manual strangulation. Her body bore over 14 injuries inflicted before her death, including severe damage to her neck, face, and genitals. Notably, her broken glasses, found near her body, became a symbol of the violent struggle she endured during the attack. This devastating incident triggered protests from the medical community, demanding justice for Dr. Moumita and calling for improved safety in hospitals.

I wrote this poem on 15th August- our Independence Day, when everyone was celebrating the glory of the freedom that we achieved but I mourned for the freedom we lost. By this poem, I tried to encapsulate the flip side of the glory.

It deeply pains me to say that unfortunately I was right, justice is still served this way…

6. Pink or Blue?

Gender equality, for how long do I have to hear about this?
Alas! I am lost in this abyss
I have been listening to it for ages
Still, we are here, stuck building each other's cages!
As a young girl, it was my sole dream and passion
Along the way, I have lost all compassion
Sick and tired of seeing people fighting over it
Believing misconceptions bit by bit
Was it just a utopian vision of my mind?
Or has the society gone blind?
Is this world just full of liars?
Preaching gender equality but practicing bias?
Why do I need to beg for respect?
Why is there fear in every aspect?
When justice is shackled by chains
Humanity cries unable to express its pain
Was it so hard to find peace in our diversity?
Equality seems like antiquity!
Yes, we have made progress a fact that I embrace
But since when did it become an egoistic race?
I feel the urge to just stop and pause
To question what if we are fighting the wrong cause,
It was never about the fight between the two

Rather about having equal worth in what we do
To wipe the tears of despair
A world so fair that everyone can dare,
Where the judgemental mindset fails
Where me, myself and my talent prevails
Where we realize feminism is not a threat to men
Patriarchy is cruel to all, not just women
Where we quench the thirst of our internal screams,
Where both boy and girl can share the same dream
Where I don't have to follow what I have been told
Where my gender does not imply that I am weak or bold
We are gender isn't a factor in deciding my salary or my worth
A world where girls are not killed after birth!
Where a boy can be creative and a girl can be brave
An equitable world is all I crave
And then my childhood dream would come true
A world not broken between *pink or blue.*

I wrote this poem because I felt very frustrated and confused by the idea of gender in our society, it makes me question a thousand things, and all I find is irony. Pink and Blue symbolize the fixed notions and stereotypes imposed by society on us. If I continue to rant about how gender equality prevails in our society building social barriers for none other than ourselves only, we all will get bored because who doesn't know about this? Everybody does, but it simply doesn't matter to anyone. We are sick and tired of this issue the results are quite disproportionate to our efforts, I wonder if we have given up hope?

{Disclaimer: I have mentioned in the poem about the 2 genders depicting it by pink and blue but this doesn't imply that there are only 2 genders in this world, it was simply a poetic adaptation with no intention to hurt or harm anyone's belief or identity}

7. In Pursuit of the Real Religion

A wise man once said,
"You may destroy the temples, mosques, and everything besides
But don't destroy the heart as that is where God resides"
God's name is all around
but the real religion is no longer found
You and me aren't we the same?
then why divide humanity in God's name,
Everyone has God within
But ironically equality seems like a sin
Religion, a term that echoes my mind
Quite intriguing, I wonder what I'll find
I expected to find sacred threads of connection
In hopes of understanding the almighty and his ways of showing affection
Alas! All I could find was unholy business in the name of the divine
Riots, violence, bloodshed and all other sins intertwined
These beliefs are like a wrecked dark storm
Almighty is one but we quarrel about his forms
In this superficial world, we are no less than a traitor
As we have forgotten the true meaning of our creator!

The sanctity of spirituality has been breached
A chasm divides what we practice and what is preached
It is the god to whom we should pray not the symbols and illustrations
Why do we make religion such a complication?
I am sure the Supreme Power is intrigued by the facade of our spirituality
In the process of defining God, we humans lost our humanity

Going against god's teachings to attain enlightenment, I admire the irony of the world.

Amongst all the poems, writing about Religion definitely felt a bit out of place but it is also one of the things I question about this world. I am very well self-aware that I am not the most religious person on this planet and neither am I a guru or source of unlimited knowledge, I am just a 15-year-old girl trying to seek answers. I don't even know if God actually exists but it is very comforting to believe in something, to believe that some supreme power exists beyond everybody on this earth, a power that will provide justice for those who seek it.

I am just bewildered by the fact that in the name of religion, we are committing horrendous sins. Religion teaches us that we should live in harmony, all creatures are our family, and it gives us a sense of brotherhood, peace and unity. It is supposed to give us a direction in life and guide us through the rights and wrongs.

Alas, we are causing wars, riots, violence, bloodshed, and partitions all in the name of god. The so-called 'divine preachers of religion' are fooling people, stealing their money and hurting their sentiments all while preaching how the materialistic world is a waste of time. Humans are discriminating against humans based on some set of beliefs, I am afraid that in the pursuit of the almighty, we have lost our humanity.

8. I Don't Know

I don't know what is going to come my way
I don't know what to do, what to say
All I know is that inside me, emptiness prevails
Self-doubt taunts me what if I fail?
Everything seems to be torn apart
Not too close to the end but so far from the start
Somewhere stuck between hopes and expectations
Hustling, with no motivation...
I don't know how to end the poem neither I knew how to start
All I know is that everything seems to be falling apart...

This is a pretty random piece of poetry that I wrote because honestly most of the time I simply don't know what I am doing and everything seems to be going off track. There is this constant feeling of being stuck in the middle with no purpose and this feeling makes me question everything circling back to the conclusion that I don't know anything.

9. The Devil's Victory?

Is this the same me or the same world?
or has everything burned?
The lessons I learned lifelong
were proved to be wrong
I thought it was better to have beauty and grace
But the world taught me to sink into the dark haze
In front of me, two paths lay
Shall I choose the darker way?
As when I was on the right trail
The world declared me frail
In a world where being bad and rude is considered as cool
I started to question everything and simply felt like a fool
All the truths were declared as lies
All I could do was sit and sigh
I was taught to believe in the illumination of light
but at the fore, I could see a different sight
I was different because I had the 'good' in me
but I was excluded, and that was all I could see
I now wanted to seek validation
Left with voids filled with desperation
I thought it was better to resent myself than to fight the world
Oh! look how the tables have turned
Should I let the darkness creep up and make an intrusion?

to save me from this exclusion
Should I leave my glory?
to celebrate *The Devil's Victory?*
Is this the same me or the same world?
or has everything burned?

I wrote this poem in class 9 and I remember all the instances very clearly and vividly. Class 9th felt like a grey year. Schools had just opened up after the lockdown, so socially I was a 6th grader in 9th class. Class ninth really changed my perspective of life, the transition from a child to a teenager can only be perfectly described by the word 'awkward'.

But this poem isn't about that, it is about the peer pressure I faced, the conflicting morals, the desire to get accepted, desperation, and the validation. 9th was the start of all my insecurities and the loss of childhood.

And no it was not all darkness and despair, it was very important for my character-building. I like to believe that it was simply there just for the 'plot'.

10. Too Good to Be True

As the warmth of the sunshine, it's my face
As my hair flows with the cool breeze
I can spend all of my time in the serenity as I please
When the vivid tapestry of flowers is all that I can gaze
Spring soothes my soul as I fall into the lavender haze
Admiring the red rose beside me, oh what a Masterpiece!
Suddenly I see a gleaming drop on petals and I freeze
And now my heart is on fire completely ablaze
For it wasn't a mere, drop it was my tear
Red rose beside me but a lover's absence turned me blue
Serenity surrounds me but O the brain was so near
For, I was all alone, battling with my biggest fears
As the cold void strikes I await the spring as if I have a clue
Some stories are meant to be unfinished as they were too good
to be true

This was my first attempt at a Petrarchan sonnet,
A Petrarchan sonnet, also known as an Italian sonnet, consists of 14 lines divided into two parts: an octave and a sestet. The octave typically follows the rhyme scheme ABBAABBA (as I have used here), while the sestet can have varying rhyme schemes like CDCDCD or CDECDE or something similar. I have used CDCCDD. this form often explores contrasting themes in the octave (8 lines) and a sestet (6 lines), allowing poets to present a shift in perspective between the two sections.
In the octave, I have tried to portray the beauty of spring and emphasized the emotions of happiness, serenity, calmness and so on. While in the sestet I have depicted a deeper darker side of having a rose but no lover beside, it represents the theme of unattained love and the acceptance that desiring love seems just too good to be true

Renaissance: The Revival Of Hope

Renaissance means rebirth or revival, in this part we will witness the revival of hope. Hope has the power to guide us through our darkest storms, it gives us a sense of direction and comfort. In the first part, I question everything about this world but I realize that not all is lost, even in the darkest corners, there lies the possibility of light. In this part, I thank everyone and everything that provided me with a sense of hope, God, my parents, teachers, friends and my beloved diary and poetry.

11. God

The concept of religion seemed a bit odd
I questioned everything, but never the god
It's so comforting to believe in a supreme power
He knows what transgresses from a single second to every hour
Someone who is above all this stupid intricacies
The chasm between wrong and right he clearly sees
He will provide justice to the ones that have been wronged
Will provide me with the answers I have longed
He created the world I am questioning
I doubted him several times, a sin I am confessioning
But God has his ways
To teach lessons and help us out of this dark haze
It's easy for me to just blame
Questioning the creator who created this game
But at the end, all I want to say
That I am beyond grateful to God for showing me the way

I questioned religion, justice, social barriers, and society in my previous poems. We all are aware of the flaws in us and society, but sometimes these flaws enrage me so much, especially when justice is at stake. It feels unbearable to witness. Yet, in the midst of that rage, God stands as a ray of hope. This belief—that there is someone watching over us, someone who holds all the answers, there is someone who is looking over us, someone is not lost and this belief was the first stepping stone in reviving my hope in this world. There is a greater force that isn't lost, even when I feel I am.

12. My Guiding Stars

Thank you for being more than just a teacher
A guiding mentor for me and not just a preacher
For actually understanding me when life went wrong
Thank you for being at my side all along
For acting like my best friend when I needed advice
That was honestly the best paradise
Thank you for listening to my musings and rants all the time
Thank you for making our journey sublime
For making things better when life got worse
You were the only person that I could trust
Your humor made my problems go away
While your ideas always showed us a new way
With you everything is fun
I will forever be grateful for what you've done

This poem is dedicated to my parents and teachers, my guiding lights. When I felt lost, they were the ones who listened, who showed me the way when everything seemed dark. They helped me reignite the hope and strength within me, giving me the courage to rise from the ashes. It's because of them that I stayed motivated, working hard with the dream of making them proud. In moments when life felt overwhelming, they stood by me, not just as mentors but as my closest friends. For that, I am deeply grateful. They never abandoned me, never let me face the storm alone. Their unwavering support helped me through it all, that is the reason I call them my guiding stars

13. Strangers to Friends

What friendship actually means we may or may not ever know
But all I know is that it is forever supposed to grow,
On you guys, I bestow my utmost trust
You have seen me in my best and the worst,
From crying to laughing because of the stupidest shit,
We are the pieces of a puzzle that perfectly fit,
Sometimes I want to hug you and throw you off a cliff at the same time
Can't possibly take the risk, you are my partner in crime!
I know farewells are inevitable, but I never want this to end
Till my grave, I will narrate the legend of how we went from strangers to friends

While writing this poem, I couldn't help but think about the unspoken nature of friendship—how we never really express our love for it, how it's just understood, taken for granted. Friendship is always in the air, making life colorful, happy, and full of laughter. My friends patiently listen to me when I yap, and for that, I'm deeply grateful. I know they'll laugh at this poem, probably call it boring, because that's their job—to roast me. And honestly, I love them for it.

14. From The Depths of a Diary

For some, I am a mere collection of sheets
For some, I am their heartbeat
As cliché as it sounds, it is the reality
I am a dimension beyond rationality
I am a poet's muse
so overwhelmed with emotions, oh god it's diary abuse!
Talking about my owner, oh dear lord he rants…
But I am an attentive listener not some nonchalant
Paper has more patience than people, it's true
I have the ability to free the people from the blue
Poets bleed on my paper
I am their creation they are my creators

This poem is written from the perspective of my diary. When talking about rebirth and the revival of hope, it would be a crime not to mention my diary. Writing in my diary has always been therapeutic—it's where I truly pour my heart out. There's something incredibly satisfying about bleeding my thoughts onto paper, releasing everything I can't say out loud. I deeply relate to Anne Frank's words: paper has more patience than people. If my diary could come alive, I know it would express it's frustration at how much I rant. But even with all the complaints, my diary will always be there as my silent, loyal companion.

15. Veer Ras!

Veer Ras! The courage that lies within us
A blazing fire, fierce and wondrous,
A profound strength, concealed in the heart's abode,
The fiery light, our guiding light on life's road.
When we think about courage, we think of the heroes of the nation
The ones who sacrificed everything without hesitation
A soldier fighting his fight
Or a policeman protecting us day and night
Tales of valor surface as time flows,
Yet, is this all that valor bestows?
Is courage merely bound to national fight,
Or does it flourish in daily duties, shining bright?
When we think about courage, we don't think about the common mass
A big mistake, alas!
For valor resides not just in the limelight's span,
But also within the heart of every common man.
It takes courage to refuse the comforts that we get
This courage is often overlooked yet
It takes courage to be bold
To not just follow what is told
Only the valiant dare to face the truth's light,

While idle souls watch, veiled from its might.
It is the work of a feeble to accept the bribe
But only the honest ones get their names inscribed
Courage lies within every citizen who chooses the nation over the pleasure
They are our nation's invaluable treasure.
It's not only the army that makes the nation proud
True courage dwells in the common crowds
For every citizen that resides on this auspicious land
Hides a veer inside them so grand!
Patriotism flows in every drop of their blood
Filled passion to rise with courage, empathy and brotherhood
Courage lies in the power of people and not just people in power
Embodied with valor, a force to empower.

This poem is about the courage that resides within every citizen. In many of my previous poems, I've criticized society—highlighting corruption and the absence of justice. But I want to acknowledge the courage that often goes unnoticed. It's not just the soldiers on the frontlines who are brave, but also the ordinary people who refuse to take a bribe, who remain honest in their duties, who choose to stand by their morals. These individuals, too, are Veer—true warriors. Amidst a world full of societal evils, there are people who have the strength to do what is right. This poem is an appreciation of their quiet, yet profound courage.

16. Beneath The Bare Bark

I was cherishing the serenity of the high mountains
The cool breeze, dreamy view and the light rain
It felt like pure bliss
But there was something I couldn't help but notice
Among the lush green coniferous pine trees, there was a tree that caught my eye
It stood still, so proud yet shy
It was a colossal tree
Soaring so high and free
But it had no leaves just the bare bark
Old, rusty, dry and full of marks
Surrounded by viridescent vegetation it was the only one left alone
Just a piece of wood standing lifeless like a stone
A thought emerged in my mind, was it feeling shame
For being different and not the same?
Was it insecure of its bare bark and marks
Had the tree lost its spark?
Did he also feel the seclusion?
Was he also craving the inclusion?
Did he also compare himself with others around?

But when I saw the tree I didn't feel pity as it was standing so proud
His uniqueness was beyond the norm
He wasn't complaining but embracing his form
The greenery around him didn't bother him at all
Even though everything was blooming, he experienced a beautiful fall
It was the tree's bare bark that enhanced the other trees around
He just stood there strongly anchoring the ground
It gave me a message that can't be forgotten
The message was to embrace the uncommon
This message was strong enough to pull me out of the dark
Sometimes, all you need to do is to look *beneath the bare bark*

I wrote this poem during a family trip to a hill station when I noticed a coniferous pine tree. It stood out—dry, barren, and stripped of leaves—surrounded by lush, green vegetation. While everything around it seemed to thrive, this tree looked almost lifeless. Out of curiosity, I wondered—does this tree feel a sense of insecurity, the way we often do when we compare ourselves to others? Does it question its purpose, or is there more to it than meets the eye?

The title Beneath the Bare Bark reflects that idea—there's so much more beyond appearances that we fail to understand. Though the tree seemed bare, it wasn't useless. It was simply in a different phase, destined to bloom in its own time. Unlike us, the tree didn't feel insecure or out of place; it embraced itself fully. It didn't seek acceptance or feel desolation—it was content in its own season. Nature accepted it just as it was, and in that, the tree found its quiet strength.

17. The Spring of Self-Acceptance

A bud looking so withered and dead
Lying amongst nature's masterpiece
For it was spring, everyone dancing to the rhythm of the cool breeze
Alas! Amongst this elegant aura, I am counting the tears the bud has shed
"I am a late bloomer", with agony she expressed
She is the odd one everyone bloomed with ease
Pleading to God she begged, "I deserve a chance please"
She had hoped to bloom; she didn't cry she bled
As the cold night passed, God must've heard her cry
Cause now she bloomed, the garden filled with fragrance
Even though she was a flower she felt like a butterfly
Cherishing this miracle, she admired her elegance in the spring sky
"All buds bloom at different times" a lesson she will always reminisce
For, spring brings hope and a feeling of self-acceptance

This poem is a Petrarchan sonnet that follows the traditional rhyming scheme, once again drawing a lesson in self-acceptance from nature. In my previous poem, I used a tree as a metaphor. This time, it's about a bud that hasn't yet bloomed, while every other flower around it has blossomed beautifully. Much like the barren tree amidst lush vegetation, this bud feels isolated and incomplete. It bleeds, cries, and longs to bloom. The bud is personified in this sonnet But after a cold, dark night, there's a ray of hope. It's as if God has heard its silent cries, and now the bud has finally blossomed. The garden is filled with its fragrance, and the bud feels a joy it had never known before. In that moment, it realizes something profound—all buds bloom at different times. The spring, depicted in the first part of the sonnet, symbolizes hope and renewal, but the bud couldn't feel that until it bloomed. By the end, spring becomes not just a season, but a revelation—a time for self-acceptance and understanding that everyone's journey to bloom is unique.

18. Lost Amidst the Storm

Clouds darker than my thoughts, skies full of thunder
What was behind those sore eyes, one could only wonder,
Eyes filled to the brim with tears
Heart caged inside the walls of fear
Even though the storm shattered me, left me feeling lost
Questioning each decision, measuring each hidden cost,
I still thank this disaster, for it helped me reform
Ironically, I found my lost soul amidst the storm...

The last poem, Lost Amidst the Storm, is a conclusion to my entire book. Though the poem is brief, its meaning runs deep. It speaks of being engulfed in dark clouds—feeling lost, hazy, questioning everything I once believed in. There's a storm raging around me, and I battle it just as you might have done someday. In the midst of this storm, I feel sad, frustrated, and uncertain about every decision I've made. But strangely, I am grateful for this chaos. It is through this storm that I reformed.

Ironically, it was in this storm that I found my lost soul. This poem embodies the purpose of my book. It's a reminder that no matter how many challenges or doubts we face, there is always a rebirth of hope. The storms in life are not there to defeat us but to help us rediscover ourselves. Sometimes, you have to get lost to truly find who you are

About The Author

Naisha Kaur, a 15-year-old student currently in the 11th grade, has been passionate about poetry for as long as she can remember. Writing has always been her way of escaping reality and diving into the world of imagination. Even though *Lost in the Abyss of Thoughts* is her fourth book, it feels like her first—because this time, she has poured her heart and soul into every word.

Naisha thrives on creative endeavors, always seeking purpose through peotic expressions. For her, poetry isn't just a hobby; it's a way to make sense of life's complexities and find peace amidst the chaos. She hopes that this book resonates with readers and helps them feel a little less alone on their own journeys.

www.ingramcontent.com/pod-product-compliance
Lightning Source LLC
LaVergne TN
LVHW090128160826
845673LV00015B/1114

* 9 7 9 8 8 9 5 8 8 8 5 2 0 *